# Rollin'

# Big Rigs

by Jay Schleifer

C A P S T O N E   P R E S S
M A N K A T O

# C A P S T O N E　　P R E S S
## 818 North Willow Street • Mankato, MN 56001

Printed in the United States of America.

*Library of Congress Cataloging-in Publication Data*
Schleifer, Jay.
    Big rigs/by Jay Schleifer
    p. cm.
    Includes bibliographical references and index.
    Summary: Describes the evolution of the big rig since its beginning in 1804, the various kinds of trucks, their key parts, driver preparation, and work rules.
    ISBN 1-56065-373-6
    1. Tractor trailer combinations--Juvenile literature. [1. Tractor trailers. 2. Trucks.]
TL230.15.S35 1996
629.224--dc20

                        95-43911
                           CIP
                           AC

Photo credits
Peter Ford: 4-10, 12, 14, 18-38, 42
Cheryl Blair: cover, 11, 16, 40

# Table of Contents

Words in **boldface** type in the text are defined in the Glossary in the back of this book.

# Chapter 1

# Truckers and Big Rigs

Many people drive to work. For a trucker, driving is the work.

A long-haul trucker could be 500 miles (800 kilometers) away from home by the end of the day. In two days, a trucker might be halfway across the country.

The long-haul trucker drives a big rig. Sometimes the big rigs are called 18 wheelers. Sometimes they are called semis.

The trucks are as big as a house. And they cost as much as a house. They crisscross the nation's highways delivering goods of all kinds.

**Big rigs are also known as semis or 18 wheelers.**

# Chapter 2

# The First Big Rig

The first truck to carry a big load was built in 1804. It was made by Oliver Evans in Philadelphia. He needed a way to move a huge steam-powered machine.

Evans put wheels under the machine and hooked the steam engine to the wheels. He drove the machine away. The first truck was born.

## Steam and Electric Trucks

In the 1800s, steam engines were put on farm tractors. They were called **traction engines**.

At the end of a day, many truckers are far away from home.

One of the makers of traction engines was International Harvester. In 1907, the company made a big truck that carried cargo. It was called the Auto-Wagon.

Steam trucks were hard to drive. They were expensive to run. Electric trucks were tried but the batteries only lasted a short time. The trucks could only make short trips. A better engine was needed.

## The Mack Brothers

In the 1890s, two brothers from Brooklyn, New York, built a better engine. The brothers, John and Augustus Mack, built an internal combustion engine. It burned gasoline or **diesel** fuel.

In 1915, the brothers founded a company called Mack Trucks. They made a truck called the Bulldog. The driver sat in a **cab** open to the weather. The wheels were turned by a chain like on a bicycle. The tires were solid rubber.

**John and Augustus Mack founded the famous Mack Truck company in 1915.**

The ride was rough. The Bulldog was built for 24 years. It made the saying "Built like a Mack Truck" famous.

## Trucking Takes Off

Many Macks were sold to the army during World War I (1914-1918). The military wanted more trucks than Mack could make. Other companies entered the truck market.

Two trailers hooked to a single tractor is called a tandem.

New trucks are streamlined to save on fuel costs.

By the mid-1920s, many different companies made trucks. More than 3 million rigs rolled down North American roads.

## The Road System and Trucks
The trucking industry and the road system have grown together. Trucking grew a lot in the

1930s. That was when the first modern highways replaced dirt roads.

Trucking grew again in the 1950s when the first interstate highways were built. The four-lane highways let trucks move along at a steady pace.

**The trucking industry and the road system have grown together.**

Roads kept getting better. So did trucks. Engines became more powerful and used less fuel. Newer trucks were built of lighter and stronger materials. Tires got better. And cabs were made more comfortable for the drivers.

# Chapter 3
# Kinds of Tractor-Trailers

Most big rigs are tractor-trailers. The power section is called the tractor. The cargo section is called the trailer. The two sections hook together.

There are two kinds of tractors. They are conventional tractors and cab-over-engine tractors.

## Conventional Tractors

Conventional tractors have long hoods that stretch out in front of the cab. Many drivers and mechanics like them the best.

**Conventional tractor engines are easy to work on.**

Drivers like the big engine in front. It provides protection if a truck should crash. Mechanics like conventional tractors because the engine is easy to work on.

Drivers also like the big sleeper behind the cab. The sleeper compartment has a bed where the driver can sleep. The drivers can easily walk in and out. They can stand up inside it.

## Cab-Over-Engine Tractors

Tractors with flat noses are cab-over-engine tractors, or cab-overs. Trucking companies prefer this type of tractor. The cab-overs take up less room in tight parking lots than other trucks. They can pull long loads.

The cab tilts up when a mechanic or driver needs to get at the engine. The sleeper is small. It is on top of the motor. It has less room and is noisier than a conventional sleeper.

**Tractors with flat noses are called cab-over-engine tractors or cab-overs.**

**Household goods are hauled in a moving van.**

## Different Types of Trailers

The type of trailer a trucker uses depends on the load. The **van** trailer can haul many different things. Most vans are about 40 feet (12 meters) long and 13 feet (390 centimeters) high. They can carry a load that weighs up to 20 tons (18 metric tons). The load can be anything from furniture to footballs.

## The Reefer Van and the Moving Van

Food that can spoil is hauled in a **reefer van**. This trailer is like a refrigerator on wheels. A motor on the front of the reefer keeps the air inside cold. The motor is powered by gas.

Household goods are hauled in a moving van. It is low to the ground. This makes it easy to load and unload.

Springs under a trailer soften the ride. This protects valuable items from breaking.

**Walls inside a tanker keep the load stable.**

### The Tanker

If the load a truck carries is liquid or gas, a **tanker** trailer is used. Tankers are shaped like a tube. They carry everything from fuel oil to milk. Tankers used to haul milk are made of stainless steel. They are shiny like a mirror.

Tankers are hard to drive. The load sloshes around and throws off the truck's balance. Walls inside the tanker slow down the sloshing. The walls are called baffles.

Tankers can carry flammable loads. When they do, a sign is placed on the back of the truck. The sign is shaped like a diamond.

Numbers printed on the signs are a code. The code tells firefighters what is inside the tanker. Then they know what to do if the truck is involved in an accident.

## The Flatbed Trailer and Cargo Trucks

When a load is too big to fit in a van, a flatbed trailer is used. Flatbeds are platforms

**Tankers carry liquids from fuel oil to milk.**

on wheels. They carry large machinery. The
loads are chained down. Sometimes they are
covered with a tarp.

**Low-boy** flatbeds carry construction gear
such as bulldozers. The low platform makes the
heavy gear easier to load and unload.

Cargo container trucks carry special metal
boxes. These boxes fit on railroad cars. They
fit in the holds of ships. They fit inside cargo
aircraft.

This way of moving goods is called
**intermodal** shipping. It is used when loads

**Low-boy trailers carry construction gear.**

need to be carried across the ocean and then over land.

## The Car Carrier and the Bobtail

The car carrier is a trailer that holds up to 13 cars and trucks. It takes the vehicles from the factories that made them to the dealers that sell them. Sometimes a small car is even put on top of the tractor.

A bobtail is a shortened tractor. It is used to move wide loads like mobile homes. The homes can be up to 60 feet (18 meters) long and a full traffic lane wide.

When a load is that big, the law requires cars with signs to drive in front of and behind the truck. The signs warn other drivers that a wide load is moving down the road.

### Other Trailers

Some states allow double trailer rigs, called **double bottoms** or **tandems**. They are made up of two trailers hooked to a single tractor.

Loads that are too big for vans go on flatbed trailers.

The rear trailer has wheels at both ends. It is hooked to the front trailer by a tow bar.

A few western states allow triple rigs. They are three trailers hooked to one tractor.

The biggest rigs on the road are in Australia. These rigs are called **road trains**. Three full trailers are hooked to a big truck. A road train may have up to 46 wheels. It can be 150 feet (45 meters) long and can weigh 130 tons (117 metric tons).

# Chapter 4

# Truck Parts

Truck makers get parts from many different companies. Then they build the trucks and put their own names on them. Popular truck makers are Kenworth, Peterbilt, Mack, GMC, Ford, and International.

Trucks with different names might have the same kinds of parts. The main parts of a truck include the engine, gears, drive shaft, brakes, suspension, hookups, bodies, computers, and radios.

**The cab is a trucker's home away from home.**

## Diesel Engines

Most tractors have diesel engines with six or eight **cylinders**. Diesel fuel is pumped into the cylinders. Pistons are inside the cylinders. When the fuel explodes, it pushes the pistons down. The motion of the pistons turns a series of parts connected to the wheels.

Diesel fuel is different from gasoline. It is heavy and sooty. Black smoke often trails from trucks that use diesel fuel.

Diesel engines are hard to start. Because the fuel is so heavy, it can become like jelly if it gets too cold. In the winter, some drivers let their engines run all night. A running engine keeps the fuel warm and fluid.

Diesel engines are very strong. They can run 250,000 miles (400,000 kilometers) and just be broken in. A car engine driven that far is often broken down.

## Gears and Drive Shafts

Gears are in the transmission. Every gear is a different speed. Many trucks have 10 speeds.

**The sleeper is a bed for the driver.**

Some have 13. Some trucks even have more than one reverse gear.

Tractors often have two **drive shafts**. They are called **twin screws**. Each shaft goes to four wheels. That means eight tires get power from the engine. When a big rig is pulling many tons of cargo up a hill, twin screws are needed.

## Suspension

The first trucks used metal springs to support the loads. Big rigs today use air. A pump on the engine pushes air into large rubber bags. The bags fit under the trailer.

The bags are like super balloons that soak up road shocks. The driver can put more air into the bags for heavy loads. The driver can take air out for lighter loads. Drivers adjust the amount of air in the bags to get a more comfortable ride.

## Brakes

Most big rigs have air brakes. When a driver steps on the truck's brake pedal, air pushes the brake shoes. The shoes rub against metal drums

**Safe truckers check their tires for cuts or bubbles.**

on the wheels. The wheels stop rolling, and the truck stops.

Each wheel has a brake. Sometimes a big rig will hiss when it starts moving. The hiss is the sound of air being let out of the brakes.

Some trucks use the Jacob's brake, or Jake. This brake uses engine power to slow the truck. If a truck makes loud noises and blows puffs of black smoke when it moves downhill, it has a Jake brake.

## Trailer Hookup

The **fifth wheel** hooks the tractor and trailer together. It is the flat metal plate on the rear of a tractor. It catches and locks a metal pin on the trailer. The pin is called a kingpin.

Fifth wheels are covered with a layer of grease. The grease allows the trailer to slide across the fifth wheel when the truck turns.

## Sleek Bodies

Old trucks were big and blocky. A lot of fuel was needed to push them along against the pressure of the air. So trucks have become

**The fifth wheel hooks the tractor and trailer together.**

more streamlined. Even long-nose conventional trucks now have sloping hoods.

At first, drivers made fun of these new trucks. They called the trucks anteaters. But when they saw how much fuel the new trucks saved, the truckers stopped making fun of them and started driving them.

**Computers tell trucking company fleet managers where their trucks are.**

Many tractors also have a sloping panel on top of the cab. The panel lets air pass over the truck easily. The truck does not have to work as hard to move, which helps save fuel.

## Computers

On-board computers help truck engines run more smoothly. They help gears shift better. They can also help drivers find their way.

Computers get signals from satellites in space to show where a truck is on a map.

Computers tell trucking company fleet managers where their trucks are. If a truck is not where it should be, the manager can call the trucker. Most truckers have beepers or cellular phones. Some trucks have fax machines on board.

## The CB Radio

Drivers use **CB** radios to talk to other truckers. CB stands for citizen's band. A CB radio is like a telephone between trucks.

Truckers share road conditions. They tell each other when they see highway patrol cars. Sometimes they just chat.

Truckers use special words on the CB. The language is almost like a secret code. Every trucker has a nickname called a handle. Highway patrol officers are called smokies or bears.

In the 1970s, truckers made CB radios popular with car drivers, too. It was only a fad, though. Few cars have CB radios today.

# Chapter 5

# Safe Trucking

Safety experts believe that 1,000 deaths a year are caused by sleepy truck drivers. When drivers fall asleep at the wheel, their trucks may run off the road. Sometimes the trucks run into other vehicles.

Laws have been passed to make trucking safer. Drivers cannot work more than 60 hours a week. They cannot drive for more than 10 hours in a row without taking eight hours off to rest. A driver may spend the rest time in the sleeper while someone else drives.

**Safety experts believe that 1,000 deaths a year are caused by sleepy truckers.**

**Safe drivers look over their hoses every time they stop.**

Drivers have to keep a record that shows when they drove and when they rested. The record is called a log. Safety officials can check a trucker's log anytime.

## Tires and Lug Nuts

Safe truckers always keep the right amount of air in their tires. They check the air pressure every day.

They look closely at the tires. They check for cuts or bubbles. If there is anything wrong with a tire, they replace it.

Truckers make sure their tires have enough tread to grip the road. If the tires are too worn, they might lose hold of the road when it rains or snows.

Lug nuts keep the wheels on a truck. The wear and tear of heavy loads and uneven highways can make the nuts come loose. Safe drivers check them every day.

## Fluids, Hoses, and Regular Checkups

Hoses bring air and fluids to a truck's brakes, air bags, and other parts. A leak in a hose can cause a truck's brakes to fail. Safe drivers look over their hoses every time they stop.

Trucks need regular checkups by a mechanic. They change the oil regularly. They rotate the tires. Drivers know that a truck that runs well is a safe truck.

## Chapter 6

# Becoming a Trucker

Almost every truck driver goes to a special school. The students spend three weeks in a classroom before they get into a truck. Then they spend nine weeks in a learning truck. A teacher sits next to them.

Truck driver students take a final exam with a written test and a driving test. Students who pass the tests get a commercial driver's license.

Most truckers are paid for the number of miles they drive. They are on the road as many hours as the law allows. They work on

**Some truckers sell their houses and hit the road until they retire.**

**Truckers have to worry about bad road conditions caused by ice and snow.**

weekends because the traffic is lighter then and they can travel farther.

## A Trucker's Life

Truckers spend many hours staring at a white line on a highway. Truckers worry about bad road conditions caused by ice and snow.

They deal with rain and fog and desert heat. They have to know what to do if their truck breaks down in the middle of nowhere.

Truckers have their favorite radio shows and listen to music from coast to coast. They also have their favorite gas stations, truck stops, and restaurants across the country.

Both men and women can be truckers. Trucking is an equal-opportunity job. It is common to see married couples trucking as a team. Some truckers sell their houses and hit the road until they retire.

Trucking is a high-stress job. Drivers can face hours of boredom. They can run into danger at any time. Many truckers miss their families back home.

But most truck drivers enjoy driving on the open road. They would not think of doing anything else. They love what they do.

# Glossary

**cab**—the part of a truck with doors and a roof over the driver and passengers

**CB**—two-way radio used to talk between vehicles

**cylinder**—can-shaped areas of an engine that hold the pistons where gas is ignited

**diesel**—type of internal combustion engine or the fuel used in this engine

**double bottoms**—twin trailers pulled by the same tractor

**drive shafts**—long rods that connect the engine to the wheels

**fifth wheel**—flat plate and hook system used to attach trailer to tractor

**intermodal**—method of shipping freight by combinations of ship, truck, and rail

**low-boy**—low flatbed used for hauling construction equipment and other odd loads

**reefer van**—refrigerated truck used for hauling food

**road trains**—extra long rigs with many trailers, used in Australia

**tandems**—twin trailers pulled by the same tractor

**tanker**—tube-shaped trailer used for hauling liquids and gases

**traction engine**—steam-powered farm tractor of the later 1800s

**twin screws**—double drive axles on a tractor

**van**—large, box-shaped trailer

# To Learn More

**Magee, Doug.** *Trucks You Can Count On.* New York: Dodd, Mead, 1985.

**Maifair, Linda Lee**. *18-Wheelers.* Mankato, Minn.: Capstone Press, 1991.

**Nentl, Jerolyn Ann.** *Big Rigs.* Mankato, Minn.: Crestwood House, 1983.

**Sheffer, H.R.** *Trucks.* Mankato, Minn.: Crestwood House, 1983.

**Stephen, R.J.** *The Picture World of Trucks.* New York: Franklin Watts, 1989.

# Useful Addresses

**American Trucking Association**
2200 Mill Road
Alexandria, VA 22314

**Independent Truckers and Drivers
  Association**
1109 Plover Drive
Baltimore, MD 21227

**Professional Truck Drivers Institute
  of America**
8788 Elk Grove Boulevard, Suite 20
Elk Grove, CA 95624

**Transportation Association of Canada**
2323 Saint Laurent Boulevard
Ottawa, ON K1G 4K6
Canada

# Index